T0009918

Copyright @ 2021 by John R. Brown and Brian J. Wright
ISBN: 978-1-5271-0699-4
Published by Christian Focus Publications Ltd
Geanies House, Fearn, Tain, Ross-shire IV20 1TW www.christianfocus.com

This edition published in 2021.
Cover illustration and internal illustrations by Lisa Flanagan
Cover and internal design by Lisa Flanagan
Printed and bound in Turkey

All rights reserved. No part of this publication may be reproduced, stored in a retrieval system,
or transmitted, in any form, by any means, electronic, mechanical, photocopying, recording or
otherwise without the prior permission of the publisher or a licence permitting restricted copying.
In the U.K. such licences are issued by the Copyright Licensing Agency, 4 Battlebridge Lane,
London, SE1 2HX. www.cla.co.uk

Zephaniah's hero

John Brown
Brian Wright

CF4•K

"It's a boy!"

The excited parents announced.

"And we're naming him **Zephaniah—'the Lord hides'**—
because we're asking the good Lord to hide him from harm."

Zephaniah needed these prayers, for he was born during
the dark, dangerous days of King Manasseh,
who encouraged God's people to break God's rules.

When Zephaniah grew up, God sent him to warn
his people that judgment was coming.

"**The Day of the Lord** is coming!
The day when the Lord judges the whole world!

In that day God will sweep away everything on earth,
like he did when he sent the flood in Noah's time."

"**Disobedience** has **consequences!**
And you, Judah, have been very **disobedient.**"

Judah was the tribe of Israel who lived in Jerusalem,
where God's temple was.

God's people were **worshiping idols** and bowing down
to the sun, moon, and stars.

Judah **turned their back** on God
and refused to follow him.

They put on clothes to look like their neighbors,
who **worshiped false gods.**

They **followed strange superstitions,**
like hopping over the doorstep to the temple.

They took people's money by tricking and hurting them.

Isn't that sad?

Judah used to worship God and bow down to him.
They used to obey his word and be nice to one another.

But Judah forgot that God was watching them
and didn't think he would punish them.

But they were wrong!

God sees everything we do and punishes every sin,
for he is holy.

God is also forgiving, though,
so he sent Zephaniah to warn Judah.

"Change your ways, you lazybones,
before I crush Jerusalem and knock down its walls!"

"I'll use my lantern to find whoever tries to hide, so don't
think you can escape punishment!"

"If you want to escape punishment," Zephaniah said, "Then **tell God you're sorry** for disobeying him. Seek the Lord, seek humility, and seek righteousness."

To encourage Judah to seek God, Zephaniah warned them not to seek help from their neighbors—because God was going to judge them, too.

"Don't look to the **west!** God will judge the **Philistines**—Goliath's people—and knock down their cities! Don't look to the **east!** God will punish the **Moabites** and **Ammonites** and fill their land with nettles and salt pits!"

"Don't look to the **south!** God will punish the
Ethiopians with his sword!"

"Don't look to the **north!** God will judge the **Assyrians,** and when he's done, their capital Ninevah will be empty except for some birds and wild animals!"

Then God reminded Jerusalem of their own rebellion.
"Your **princes** are roaring lions!
Your **judges** are hungry wolves!
Your **prophets** lie, and your **priests** break my laws!"

The Lord sent Zephaniah to Judah so they would
turn away from their sins and come back to God.

God knew, however, that most people would ignore him.
And since he is righteous, he will judge them. But God is also
merciful, and he promised to **set all things right** some day.

"Wait patiently, my people,

for the time when judgment's **done;**

For I will purify all speech,

so all can worship me as **one.**"

"My people will bring me gifts,

their loyalty to **prove**,

And none will feel ashamed,

for the rebels I'll **remove**."

"Everyone will be humble,
for they'll trust in the name of the **Lord**.

They'll do no wrong and tell no lies,
but live in one **accord**."

"Their daytimes will be peaceful,
their sleep all sweet at **night**;
for gone will be all evil
that might scare or cause them **fright**."

"Sing! Exult! Shout aloud!
Rejoice with all your **heart**!
For the Lord has finished judging,
and your enemies he broke **apart**!"

"The Lord—your King—will live with you;
your troubles gone at **last!**
You'll never fear disaster again,
for your problems are all **past**."

"Your loving God will be with you,
a mighty hero who **saves**!
He will joyfully delight in you,
and sing over you with **praise**!"

"I will gather those
whose hearts were sad,
when my laws
were **disobeyed.**"

"I will heal the sick,
honor the shamed,
and gather
those chased **away.**"

"On that day I'll bring you home,

and all the world will **know**,

That I forgave you and put things right,

by the blessings I'll **bestow.**"

We don't know when all this will happen, but we do know
the name of the Mighty Hero God is sending to save us...

Jesus!

Jesus came to rescue everyone who is sorry for doing bad and trusts in him as their Savior.

And Jesus is coming back again to bring all God's children home to live with him **forever**!

When you read Zephaniah, "the Lord hides," remember that
God hides from harm those who trust in him,
even when we've done bad things.

Praise God for sending Zephaniah! Praise God for sending Jesus!
Hallelujah! What a Savior!

CHRISTIAN FOCUS PUBLICATIONS

F H •K m

Christian   Christian   CF4K   Mentor
Focus   Heritage

Christian Focus Publications publishes books for adults and children under its four main imprints: Christian Focus, CF4K, Mentor and Christian Heritage. Our books reflect our conviction that God's Word is reliable and Jesus is the way to know him, and live for ever with him.

Our children's publication list covers pre-school to early teens. We also publish personal and family devotional titles, biographies and inspirational stories that children will love.

From pre-school board books to teenage apologetics, we have it covered!

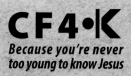

CF4•K

Because you're never
too young to know Jesus